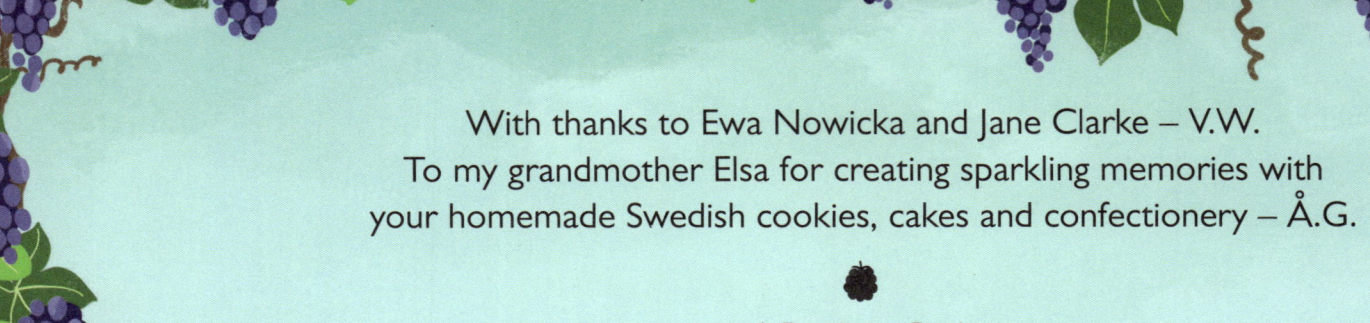

With thanks to Ewa Nowicka and Jane Clarke – V.W.
To my grandmother Elsa for creating sparkling memories with your homemade Swedish cookies, cakes and confectionery – Å.G.

A Raspberry Book
Author: Valerie Wilding
Illustrator: Åsa Gilland
Editor: Tracey Turner
Art direction and cover design: Sidonie Beresford-Browne
Design: Nicky Scott

First published 2025 by Macmillan Children's Books
an imprint of Pan Macmillan
The Smithson, 6 Briset Street, London, EC1M 5NR
Associated companies throughout the world
www.panmacmillan.com

ISBN 978-0-7534-4982-0

Copyright © Raspberry Books Ltd 2025

All rights reserved. No part of this publication may be reproduced, stored in or introduced into a retrieval system, or transmitted, in any form or by any means (electronic, mechanical, photocopying, recording or otherwise), without the prior written permission of the publisher. Any person who does any unauthorized act in relation to this publication may be liable to criminal prosecution and civil claims for damages.

1 3 5 7 9 8 6 4 2
1TR/0725/UG/WKT/140WF

EU representative: Macmillan Publishers Ireland Ltd, 1st Floor, The Liffey Trust Centre 117-126 Sheriff Street Upper, Dublin 1 D01 YC43

A CIP catalogue record for this book is available from the British Library.

Printed in China

This book is sold subject to the condition that it shall not, by way of trade or otherwise, be lent, resold, hired out, or otherwise circulated without the publisher's prior consent in any form of binding or cover other than that in which it is published and without a similar condition including this condition being imposed on the subsequent purchaser.

CONTENTS

Introduction 4

The World on a Plate 6

Injera, Ethiopia 8

Ratatouille, France 10

Tamales, Mexico 12

Poffertjes, the Netherlands ... 14

Pizza, USA 16

Koulouri, Greece 18

Odeng, South Korea 20

Plov, Uzbekistan 22

Käsespätzle, Germany 24

Bobotie, South Africa 26

Gelato, Italy 28

Idli sambar, India 30

Jerk chicken, UK 32

Wonton soup, China 34

Empanadas, Argentina 36

Barbecue, Australia 38

Bigos, Poland 40

Lovo, Fiji 42

Meze, Turkey 44

Sushi, Japan 46

Index 48

INTRODUCTION

We all need food to help us grow, and to give us the energy we need. We think about it, in one way or another, every day. Some people love cooking for family and friends, others like dreaming up recipes, and some of us just like eating! And we all have our favourite foods.

The children in this book tell you about their favourite dishes, which are all so different. While someone's eating toast for breakfast, someone else is starting the day with spicy *idli sambar*. And while one child's idea of a great snack is a tasty *empanada*, another's might be fish cakes on a stick!

Some of the dishes in this book have been part of a country's tradition for hundreds of years, while others are recent arrivals from other cultures. You might recognise many of the ingredients, but maybe they're cooked in a way that you've never seen before.

Through these pages you can discover what children like you love to eat. Maybe you'll find something you'd like to try, or even cook for yourself. So grab your fork, or your chopsticks, or maybe a piece of *injera*, and take a look . . .

INJERA, ETHIOPIA

Hello, I'm Yonas. I live in Awassa, Ethiopia with my parents, my little sister Elsabet and my two older stepsisters, Tizita and Luliya.

I'm lucky, because we have my favourite food, injera, at most meals. It's very thin flatbread, made with wheat and tiny grains called teff, mixed with water and left for three days to ferment. Mama pours some onto a large, round cooking pan, called a mitad. When the injera's cooked, it's like a pancake with little holes in.

In Ethiopia, people have been cooking injera for hundreds of years. It's useful, because it's a serving dish, eating utensil and food, all in one!

This injera fills our big blue plate. Large spoonfuls of colourful foods are heaped on it and it's set in the middle for everyone to share. There's golden yellow yater kik alicha, made from split peas, bright green collard leaf stew, and red lentils in another stew called misir wot.

There's doro wot, too – chicken stewed with ginger, garlic and a spice mix called berbere. It also has boiled eggs in it! Doro wot is too spicy for Elsabet, but I'm used to it.

I tear off bits of my own injera and pick up food with my right hand. Sometimes we perform gursha. Starting with Papa, we pick up something tasty with injera and pop it in the mouth of whoever's next to us. Gursha shows love and respect. Today Tizita did it for me, and I did it for Luliya.

YATER KIK ALICHA

DORO WOT

MISIR WOT

When the food's gone, the injera beneath is full of juices, so we share that, too. No wonder injera's my favourite food. It comes with flavours of everything!

RATATOUILLE, FRANCE

Bonjour! I'm Lina. I live in Oppède in Provence, France, with my brother, Louis, and our parents.

Every month in summer our neighbours, Monsieur Pierre and Madame Laurent, come for lunch. Papa puts a long table beneath a grapevine in our courtyard. Monsieur Pierre brings cheese and his special salad, and Madame Laurent brings a *gâteau* or a basket of *macarons* for dessert.

On Friday, after school, I help make a huge bowl of *ratatouille* (my favourite!). Maman fries onions and garlic, while I prepare aubergines, courgettes, tomatoes, and red and green peppers. Sometimes we cut them into slices, sometimes into chunks.

AUBERGINE

COURGETTE

We sauté the vegetables in oil for a few minutes, then Maman lifts them out with a huge spoon. The oil drains back into the pan through holes in the spoon, then the vegetables go in a big pot. We add salt, pepper, and herbs, like parsley, basil, thyme and bay leaves, and put it in the oven. Once the *ratatouille's* cooked, it cools overnight.

On Saturday morning, Louis and I fetch baguettes from the bakery. When we return, the table is heaped with ham, prawns, garlicky aioli sauce, salad, and pistou sauce with basil and more garlic. There are Monsieur Pierre's cheeses, too – brie and blue cheese. They're smelly, but very tasty!

GRAPEVINE

MACARONS

RATATOUILLE

Our ratatouille is full of delicious flavour. Everyone loves eating it with bread and it soon disappears. But there's some in the fridge for tomorrow's lunch boxes!

Ratatouille began as a meal for poor farmers, using leftover vegetables. It became popular in France and other countries, cooked by top chefs. It even stars in a movie . . . along with a rat!

TAMALES, MEXICO

Hola! I'm Rodrigo from Mexico City, where I live with my family. I have three sisters: Camila, Lucia and Antonia.

My uncles, aunts and cousins live in the city, too. On the first Saturday of every month, we all meet in a park called Parque Hundido for a family picnic. It's not far, and I carry a lot of the picnic stuff.

As soon as we get together with our cousins, we talk, laugh and play while the grown-ups unpack the picnic. There's lots of food, but I always have room for my favourite snack later on.

After lunch, my cousins and I see who can spot the most creatures. One point for a squirrel, two for a lizard and three for a cat. Lots of cats are looked after in Parque Hundido.

As it grows cooler, Papa calls, 'Who wants a snack?' The whole family shouts, 'I do!' but I always shout, 'Tamales!' and everyone laughs. They know they're my favourite!

We join the queue at the tamales stand and choose what we want. The warm tamales are made of corn dough, stuffed with delicious fillings. They're wrapped in the outer layer of corn cobs, called husks, to be cooked and sold.

Tamales are a traditional dish from Central and South America. They are steamed upright in a tall pot called a tamalera.

The filling I love is cheese and spinach with tomatillo sauce. Tomatillos are tangy and slightly sweet, and are cooked with peppers, onions and garlic. The melted cheese mixes with the sauce and it's spicy and gooey. A scrumptious end to our family day!

POFFERTJES, THE NETHERLANDS

Hi, I'm Anneke! I live with my mother near Hulst in the Netherlands. Every December, my grandparents – Opa and Oma – take me to the Christmas Market. This year, Daan from next door is coming, too.

We walk around the market looking at the colourful lights, the Christmas tree and the gift stalls. A band plays Christmassy songs and, every year, Opa and Oma like to stay and listen. 'Go and have fun, and bring us back some poffertjes,' they say. Every year!

Mmm, poffertjes – my favourite treat! We sniff the air as we draw near to the delicious-smelling poffertje stand.

The poffertje pan has round hollows in it. The cook holds a container full of batter, made from eggs, butter, flour, yeast, milk and sugar, all beaten together. He fills the hollows about three quarters full, and we watch as the hot poffertjes start puffing up. Little holes appear on the top, and they begin to look dry.

Poffertjes are a popular sweet treat at any festival in the Netherlands, not just at Christmas. 'Poffertje' comes from a Dutch word – pof – meaning 'puff.'

'Flip them, flip them!' Daan says. The cook flicks each poffertje over with his wooden fork, and we see how lovely and golden the little puffy pancakes have become.

POFFERTJE PAN

POFFERTJE

The cook piles our poffertjes on cardboard plates. He showers them with powdery sugar and drizzles melted butter over them. Mmm!

We sit on a bench with Opa and Oma to eat our poffertjes. They're slightly crispy outside, and airy, like a cloud, inside. Oma puts two of hers in a plastic box to take home for Mam. Opa pops one in, too. I look at Daan and we laugh. Our poffertjes are all gone!

PIZZA, USA

Hi, I'm Violetta. I live in Paterson, New Jersey, USA, with my Mom and Dad and our noisy parrot, Peanuts.

Mom's been promoted at work, so our whole family's going out for dinner to celebrate — Nonna, too. Nonna is the Italian name for grandmother, and we're part Italian. Nonna is all Italian! She loves pizza (we do, too!) so we're going to an Italian pizzeria.

My best friend Mason lives in the apartment below us and he's invited, so I bang on the floor to tell him we're on our way, and we meet by the elevator.

I used to think pizza was American, like corn dogs, and burger with fries, but pizzas were first made in Naples, Italy. When Italian immigrants came to live in the USA, they brought pizza recipes with them.

Soon, Nonna said, everyone in America came to love pizzas, and now there are pizzerias all over the world. You can buy pizza slices from stands in the street. We do that sometimes and eat them in the park.

In the restaurant we have a whole pizza each. Mason and I peep around the enormous menu to talk about what to have. His favourite is a Hawaiian, with ham, pineapple and extra mozzarella cheese. Everyone else has Margheritas, but my favourite is pepperoni, with spicy Italian sausage, mushrooms and extra mozzarella. As Nonna says, 'Deliziosa!'

The popularity of pizzas spread from Naples, Italy, in the 1800s. The Margherita is the most popular kind in the world, showing the colours of Italy's flag: red tomato sauce, white mozzarella, and green basil leaves.

Mason and I always have extra mozzarella, because it goes stringy, and we love seeing who can pull the longest string without using their hands!

KOULOURI, GREECE

Hello, I'm Iris! I live with my parents in a small town near Athens, the capital city of Greece.

My favourite meal is breakfast. On Fridays we have **spanakopita** – a crispy pie made with spinach and feta cheese. It's Dad's favourite. Sometimes we have **bougatsa**, which is a pastry filled with sweet custard or cheese. Mum loves that. On Sundays we have my favourite – tasty bread rings called **koulouris**!

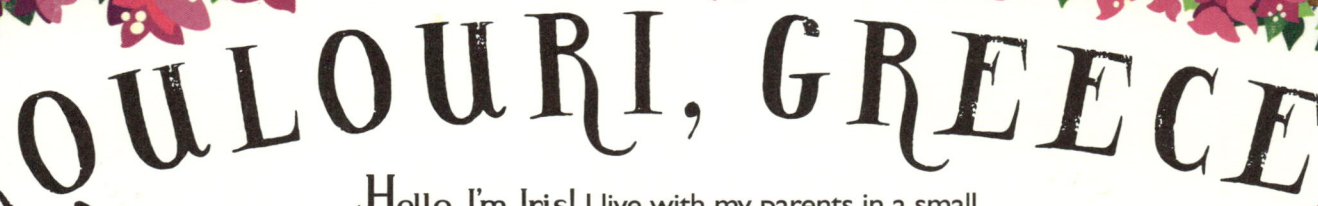

DOUGH

SESAME SEEDS

The evening before, Mum mixes the dough for the koulouris, then I roll it into long sausage shapes. I form them into circles and pinch the ends together. Before we bake them, we dip them in water then into a dish full of sesame seeds.

Koulouris are sold in the street and in all bakeries. Many people buy them on their way to work for a quick, easy and delicious breakfast.

Next morning the koulouris go back into the oven for five minutes. The toasty sesame smell makes my mouth water. While they cool on a rack, I put orange juice on the table, along with butter, yogurt, chopped nuts, jam and marmalade.

Mum and Dad drink coffee and I have juice. I drizzle golden honey over my bowl of thick, creamy yogurt, then sprinkle nuts on top. Walnuts are my favourite.

When the koulouris have cooled a little, Mum piles them on a plate and we help ourselves. A koulouri is soft and a bit chewy inside, and crispy outside. Dad slices his and spreads jam on each half. Mum dips chunks of hers in honey. I like my koulouri just as it is. I start the day feeling full of good things!

ODENG, SOUTH KOREA

Hello, I'm Ye-jun. I live with my sister, Soo-ah, and our father and auntie in Busan, South Korea.

Auntie's a dentist and works very hard. On her day off, she likes collecting us from school and, on the way home, we go through the fish market. Auntie always buys us snacks as a treat! We take turns choosing which food stand we go to.

Soo-ah skips ahead and I know exactly where she's going. 'Bungeoppang!' she cries. Bungeoppang are pastries shaped like fish, with a sweet bean filling inside, and Soo-ah adores them.

Auntie calls her back. 'It's Ye-jun's turn,' she says, and Soo-ah grins. 'That's OK,' she says. 'I like odeng, too.'

Odeng is my favourite. It's a fish cake made of mashed fish kneaded together with flour and ingredients like onions, carrots, salt and sugar. The mixture is flattened, then cut into long strips.

Seafood is very popular in South Korea. Odeng are copied from Japanese fish cakes, and the name odeng is borrowed from the Japanese word oden, which means fish cake stew.

SKEWER

ODENG

We like watching the stallholder thread the cooked strips on to a bamboo skewer, folding them so they look like pleated ribbons. Soo-ah thinks they're more like caterpillars.

BUNGEOPPANG

We have a cup of seafood-flavoured broth to dip our odeng into, but before I eat mine, I brush it with soy sauce. We sit on a wall opposite a seafood seller, watching crabs scuttling around a tank while Auntie chooses something for dinner. I enjoy the tasty fish flavour and slight sweetness of my odeng, and I drink every drop of the broth. It warms me up on a cold day like today.

PLOV, UZBEKISTAN

Hello, I'm Rasul and my sister is Sariya. We live on a fruit farm near Jizzakh, Uzbekistan. Our mother had an accident so, until she's better, she's brought us to stay with our grandparents in Samarkand. Father stayed home to look after our orchards.

Grandma's teaching us to make plov. Since we've been here we've had it twice and it's become our favourite meal. Today is Uncle Umid's birthday and he loves plov, too, so that's what we're having!

Grandma cuts lamb into cubes, and slices onions into rings. We pile the meat into an old cast iron cooking pot called a kazan. While it fries, Grandma cuts carrots into long thin sticks. The vegetables go in next, and Sariya adds cumin, coriander and paprika. I stir in barberries and some water.

KAZAN

BARBERRIES

GARLIC HEAD

I peel the papery skin from whole heads of garlic and slice off the root. The plov's already smelling good!

After a while, Grandma piles rice and boiling water on top of the meat mixture and Sariya presses the garlic heads into it. When the rice is cooked, Grandma heaps it into a mound on top of the meat.

Different versions of plou are traditionally served throughout Uzbekistan, at all sorts of occasions from small family dinners to huge wedding parties. And birthdays, of course!

I make shakarob salad, with thinly sliced onion, tomatoes and some dressing. Sariya tops it with fresh dill, just as Uncle Umid arrives. We hug him and wish him 'Happy birthday'. Then he sniffs. 'I smell plou!' he says. 'Who's been busy?' Sariya jumps up. 'Me!' she says, and everyone laughs.

SHAKAROB SALAD

PLOV

Mum smiles and says we can make plou when we go home. I bet we'll be able to make it just like Grandma's!

KÄSESPÄTZLE, GERMANY

Hello, I'm Felix, and Mila is my sister. We live in an apartment above our parents' shop in Willich, Germany.

Mila works some evenings in a restaurant, Mama plays volleyball on Wednesdays, and Papa goes swimming after work on Fridays. We're all home on Tuesdays and that's the night we eat together and watch TV.

Everyone helps to cook our favourite meal. It's called Käsespätzle – cheesy noodles! It's a perfect TV dinner because you only need a fork.

While Papa shreds Emmental cheese, the rest of us make spätzles. The food mixer stirs flour, eggs, salt, nutmeg, milk and water. When little holes start to appear in the dough, it's ready.

EMMENTAL CHEESE

NUTMEG

Mila holds the metal spätzle press over a pan of simmering water, and I spoon a big dollop of mixture into the square box on top. I press it through the holes so little worms of dough come out – spätzles! Mila slides the box back and forth and it cuts the spätzles off so they plop into the water.

Spätzles are one of Germany's most popular dishes. They have been celebrated in poems and songs, and a museum dedicated to the spätzle outgrew its home and in 2023 became a travelling exhibition.

In a few minutes, the spätzles float to the top, which means they're done. Mama lifts them out with a big spoon.

SPÄTZLE PRESS

KÄSESPÄTZLE

Papa fries onions while we put the Käsespätzle together in an ovenproof dish. A layer of spätzles, a layer of shredded cheese, more spätzles and a last layer of cheese. Into the oven it goes.

When it's ready, Papa piles crispy onions and fresh parsley on top and we settle down on the sofa to watch our favourite wildlife programme and eat Käsespätzle! Yum!

BOBOTIE, SOUTH AFRICA

Hi, I'm Zola from Cape Town, South Africa. I live with my dad, great-aunt Sadie, and my brother, Nik. Our dog, Joel, is best friends with Aunt Sadie's cat, Cupcake.

Dad's grandparents came from Malaysia to live in Cape Town. Whenever we eat my favourite meal, bobotie, he tells us that many years ago, Malay immigrants made the dish extremely popular here. He says we're still using his grandmother's recipe.

MANGO CHUTNEY

Bobotie's popularity spread to several other African countries. It's such a favourite in South Africa that it's considered to be the country's national dish.

Aunt Sadie says everyone has their own version of bobotie, but ours is best. It's spicy minced beef or lamb topped with an egg and milk mixture, then baked. It also has bread in it. I've taught Nik how to put the slices of bread in a bowl and pour a cup of milk over them. Sometimes he misses!

Dad cooks onions with spices like curry powder, turmeric, cumin and garlic. Then he adds the beef or lamb to the pan. When it's all brown, it's my turn. I add dollops of mango chutney and tomato paste, and other yummy things like sultanas, chopped apricots, lemon juice and almonds.

I wash Nik's hands and he squeezes the bread, leaving the milk in the bowl. He always says, 'Yuck!' but he loves doing it. The squished bread is mixed in with the meat, then Dad puts it in a dish. He adds the egg and milk topping and pops it in the oven.

ALMONDS

BOBOTIE

When Aunt Sadie comes home with the shopping the bobotie is golden brown and ready. She says, 'That smells wonderful!' Bobotie tastes wonderful, too – spicy, sweet, tangy and savoury all at once. Our family recipe's the best!

GELATO, ITALY

Hi! I'm Vittoria. I live with my brothers, Tommaso and Dante, and our mother and grandfather in a farmhouse near Salerno, Italy.

Three years ago, Mamma started a new business. A gelateria! She sells gelato, which is Italian ice cream. It's the best in the whole region!

We turned a barn into a gelato parlour, with a separate room where the gelato's made. People come to sit or stroll in the sun with a tasty cone, or they buy tubs of gelato to take home.

Our gelateria is always busy. Sometimes I bring friends home, and Mamma lets them choose their favourite flavour. The ones they like best are strawberry, zingy lemon and pistachio.

Everything in the gelateria is spotlessly clean, especially the machines. They do the hard work, like pasteurising ingredients to make them safe to eat, and stirring the milky, creamy mixture slowly as it freezes. Mamma and her helpers mix the different flavours that go in trays in the shop counter, which is really a giant refrigerator.

Sometimes Tommaso and I wear gloves and special hats to cover our hair, and help prepare the strawberries, cherries and lemons.

The first gelateria was opened in Paris in the 17th century by Procopio Cutò, an Italian chef. He brought his grandfather's gelato machine from Sicily.

PASTEURISER

My favourite gelato? Hmm... They all taste wonderful, but I think black raspberry is best. My grandfather grows the berries, and he loves it, too. It's sweet and tangy and a gorgeous colour. Yes, that's my favourite.

Some gelaterias serve savoury gelatos, such as tomato and basil, blue cheese, celery and cucumber, even anchovy! I wonder what flavour Mamma's planning next!

BLACK RASPBERRY

PISTACHIO

IDLI SAMBAR, INDIA

Hello! I'm Avi, from Kondotty, in the south of India. Papa is an airline flight attendant, and Mum is on leave from work because she's had a baby — my sister, Shree. Very small, very cute, and very noisy!

Mum loves cooking and she's been trying different recipes. Most of them are great. My favourite is a breakfast dish called *idli sambar*. Whenever Papa's home for breakfast, that's what we have.

TOOR DAL

TAMARIND

Sambar is a vegetable stew, made with yellow split pigeon peas called *toor dal*. They're cooked then mashed. Other vegetables, like okra, carrots and tomatoes are cooked separately. Mum adds a spice mix called *sambar* powder, and water flavoured with tamarind fruit. There's so much goodness in *sambar*!

Once the toor dal and veg are mixed together, Mum fries spices and herbs and pours it over the sambar. Next, we need idlis. They're savoury cakes made with a batter of rice and toor dal. When they're steamed, they puff up like tiny soft pillows.

Idli sambar is a delicious breakfast popular in South India. According to folk tales, it was invented in the royal household in the 1600s, perhaps by the King himself.

IDLI SAMBAR

IDLI

Some people put their idlis in the sambar, others pour sambar over their idlis, but I have my own way of eating it. I tear off a piece of idli, scoop up some sambar, and pop it in my mouth. The idli seems to melt, leaving delicious spicy, sweet and sour flavours behind! It's the best breakfast ever and definitely my favourite.

JERK CHICKEN, UK

Hey, I'm Harrison, and the boy who looks like me is my twin, Victor. We live in Birmingham, UK, with Mum, Dad, our dog, Chief, and our kitten, Beans. Chief adores Beans!

We live near Birmingham's 'curry mile', which has loads of Indian restaurants. We love Indian food, but there's something I love even more. It's from Jamaica, where Mum's family lives, and it's called jerk chicken.

The best jerk chicken we ever have is when Uncle Dane's staying. He works for Jamaican TV and sometimes visits the UK on business. He loves to cook whenever he gets the chance. Our jerk chicken is normally made using marinade from a jar, but if Uncle Dane's willing, our parents get him to make his fresh marinade. Mum says it's a true taste of Jamaica.

So Victor and I take Uncle Dane shopping to buy everything he needs, like spices, limes, cinnamon, chillies, nutmeg, ginger and spring onions. He whizzes the marinade ingredients together in the blender. It smells amazing! He lets Victor and me rub the marinade onto chicken pieces, then they're left in the fridge overnight.

Next day, Mum makes Jamaican rice-and-peas. There aren't any peas in it – they're red kidney beans, which are called peas in Jamaica. Dad helps Uncle Dane to make festivals to go with the baked chicken. Festivals are little fried cornbread rolls. Victor and I love them, especially when they're still warm.

JERK CHICKEN

RICE AND PEAS

FESTIVALS

Jerk chicken, rice-and-not-peas and festivals – definitely my favourite food!

'Jerk' is a style of cooking especially popular in Jamaica. Chicken, or another ingredient such as pork or vegetables, is coated in tasty spices and left to marinate overnight before cooking.

WONTON SOUP, CHINA

Hi, my name is Fēn, from Nanjing, China. My parents and I are happy because my stepbrother, Yǔzé is back from university.

Yǔzé always likes wonton soup when he comes home. That's lucky for me, because it's my favourite! When I was little and not feeling well, Mama gave me wonton soup to make me feel better. She calls it comfort food.

First, Mama makes chicken broth with sesame oil, ginger and garlic, then I help make the wontons. Wontons are little steamed dumplings. My favourite filling is a mixture of minced pork and chopped prawns, with soy sauce, sesame oil, ginger, and chopped spring onions.

My job is to take a small square of yellow dough, called a wonton wrapper, and put a teaspoon of filling in the middle. Mama folds them in fancy ways, but my way is easier. I wet the wrapper's edges to make the dough sticky, then fold it into a triangle. Finally I fold the two bottom corners over the filling. The wonton looks as if it's hugging itself!

WONTON WRAPPER

Mama drops the wontons into gently boiling water. When they float on top, we know they're ready. The dough becomes smooth and almost see-through, like a thin skin.

Wontons have been enjoyed in China for hundreds of years. Different ways of folding them have special names, such as fish, envelope, bonnet and diamond.

I share out the wontons between four bowls, then Mama pours the steaming chicken broth over them. Wonton soup!

CHOPSTICKS

WONTONS

CHICKEN BROTH

My spoon has a flat bottom, so it won't tip when I put it down. That's for the broth. In my left hand I have my chopsticks, for the wontons. Mmm, so yummy!

EMPANADAS, ARGENTINA

I'm Felipe, from Córdoba in Argentina. I live with my sister, Alma, and our two mums, Mama Lu and Mama Ana.

Mama Lu is a nurse, and Mama Ana works at home for a lawyer. Sometimes she has to go to court for a day. That's when Señora Garcia, our neighbour, looks after us.

We love days with Señora Garcia, especially when she takes us to the splash pad in the park. We take a bag with fruit, potato chips, water, towels and spare clothes, but we never go to the splash pad without visiting the empanada shop.

Empanadas are like semi-circular pies. Crisp pastry contains tasty meat and vegetable fillings, and sometimes fish. My favourite is the empanada Cordobesa. This is what's in it: beef, onion, garlic, paprika, tomatoes, hard-boiled egg and olives. There's also raisins and sugar! Cordobesas are savoury and sweet and none of my family like them. I love them!

Alma and I choose our empanadas, and Señora Garcia picks two because she'll take one home for Señor Garcia.

When we reach the splash pad, we pull off our shorts and T-shirts. Wearing our swim things, we run through the water fountains that spray up from the ground. There are buckets on poles that suddenly tip over and drench you. Alma likes standing in the mist spray with her face turned up.

SPLASH PAD

When Señora Garcia calls, 'Snack time!', we wrap ourselves in towels and tuck into our empanadas. I hardly say a word. I just concentrate on enjoying my favourite food.

Empanadas originally came from Spain. Each region in Argentina has their own speciality, and it's easy to tell them apart, because the pastry edge of each type is folded differently.

BARBECUE, AUSTRALIA

Hi, I'm Yarran. I live with my dads in the city of Gold Coast in Queensland, Australia. I have a sister, Ellin, and a baby brother, Miro.

We love going down to Main Beach in the late afternoon for a barbecue with our friends. It's usually my family, with Ellin's friend Olivia, and my best mates, Theo and Louie, who all come with their parents, too.

Like many beaches, Main Beach has a barbecue area, so the grown-ups get the barbie going, while the rest of us have a swim and play catch or beach cricket until they call us to come and eat.

If I could choose any meal in the world, I would pick a barbie on the beach, with the wonderful smoky aromas and sizzling sounds. We always have sausages, which we call snags. I like mine well done with crispy skin and a big squirt of barbecue sauce.

My very favourite thing is giant prawns with caramelised lemon. Dad lines up the prawns on the grill and brushes them with garlic-flavoured olive oil. While they're cooking, he grills chunks of lemon until they're charred and slightly browned. As the lemon gets charred it becomes sweeter and, when you squeeze it over the prawns, it's so delicious!

Theo's mum brings chicken and corn cobs to cook, and Louie's parents always bring salad, cauliflower kebabs and grilled cheese to the barbecue. Louie's mum is vegetarian. Everything tastes amazing in the sunshine, but those prawns are the best! Yummo!

Barbecues are so popular in Australia that barbecue cooking competitions are held all over the country, and there's even been a barbecue reality TV show.

BIGOS, POLAND

Witam, I'm Zofia! I live in Tarnów in southeast Poland with my parents, my baby sister, Luiza, and my brother, Jakub. Our grandmother, aunt, uncle and cousins have come for dinner.

Today there's a huge pot of my favourite meal in the middle of the table – a stew called **bigos**. It was made yesterday, because it tastes even better when it's been heated up again.

First we have chicken soup called **rosół z kury** – just a little, as we need to leave room for bigos! Grandma made the soup because Jakub has a cold, and **rosół z kury** is good for the sniffles.

For our **bigos**, Papa cuts up chicken, pork, bacon and chunks of Polish sausages, called **kielbasa**. Bigos is often called Hunter's Stew, and you can use any meat you like. Mama adds mushrooms, onions, fresh cabbage and **sauerkraut**, which means 'sour cabbage'. It tastes better than it sounds!

When the lid comes off the bigos pot, the aroma fills the room. Our dog Maks smells it, too, but he's not allowed food from the table. We eat bigos with rye bread and a big bowl of potatoes. Delicious!

In the past, bigos was cooked in an iron cauldron over a fire. Hunters would keep adding meat to it, so sometimes it cooked for days.

RYE BREAD

POTATOES

SERNIK

Our dessert is sernik – Mama's cheesecake with raisins in it. Even though we always have the same things with bigos, we never get tired of it. It's perfect for sharing and it's warm and comforting. All the time I'm eating it, I'm wondering if there'll be some left over for tomorrow!

Lovo, Fiji

Hello, I'm Jope! I live with my family in a small village on the Fijian island of Viti Levu. I have a sister called Lusi, and more family living close by.

Today we're celebrating my new baby cousin, Jioji! We're cooking lots of food in a lovo – an underground oven. Lovo is my favourite meal, because we share delicious food and we're all happy together.

To make the lovo, we dig a pit and put stones in the bottom. Then we pile firewood on top and burn it. After a while, the burnt wood is removed, leaving hot stones behind. The heat will cook our food.

BANANA LEAVES

LOVO

The meat, flavoured with garlic, chilli and ginger, is wrapped in banana or coconut leaves. Sometimes people like to braid the leaves. But before it goes into the lovo, sticks and more banana leaves are laid over the stones. The leaves add moisture, which makes steam to cook the meat. More leaves and a layer of old sacks go on top. That traps the steam inside the lovo.

Lovo is used for all sorts of celebrations, such as marriages and festivals. It's traditional for funerals, too, bringing everyone together.

We have palusami, too. It's a mixture of coconut cream, corned beef, onion, garlic and ginger and it's spread on big taro leaves. The leaves are rolled into fat parcels and cooked in the lovo. There'll be a fishy one for Lusi – she likes fish best.

PALUSAMI PARCELS

When all the food parcels are opened at last, the aroma is so delicious. The meat is easy to share because it's so tender it just falls apart. Lovo's worth waiting for!

TARO LEAVES

MEZE, TURKEY

My name is Elif. I live in Gaziantep, Turkey, with my parents, my brother, Deniz, and our chihuahuas, Pablo and Maya. Deniz works at the zoo.

When our friends from Istanbul visit, we spend hours talking about what everybody's been doing. Instead of an ordinary dinner, we have a huge meze – lots of little dishes for everyone to share. You help yourself from any dishes you fancy, whenever you want. It's my very favourite meal, because I eat what I like best and I don't have to eat anything I don't like.

HAYDARI

There's always crusty bread with dips. Mum makes a dip called haydari with yogurt, garlic, mint and feta cheese, but my favourite dip is muhammara. It's made with walnuts, roasted red peppers, garlic, lemon juice and spices. The flavours moosh together overnight and it's delicious.

We make dolmas, which are stuffed vine leaves. My favourite filling is rice with onions, pine nuts, tomato, mint, parsley and spices. I put dollops of filling on the leaves and roll them up tightly. Then we cook the dolmas in lemony water.

Meze can be a whole meal, like the one Elif describes, or a few dishes can be served as a starter before a main course. It's popular in many other countries as well as Turkey.

There's always cheese and melon and little meatballs called kofte ... there are so many tasty things, it's no wonder this is my favourite meal!

FRIED SQUID

KOFTE

TARATOR

MUHAMMARA

DOLMAS

We often have fried squid with tarator – that's yogurt, walnut and garlic sauce. Deniz loves pickled sardines, so we save some for him. He's usually home late from the zoo, so he quickly showers then tucks into lamb studded with pistachio nuts, salad and – of course – pickled sardines.

SUSHI, JAPAN

Hello, I'm Ema, and I live in an apartment in Osaka, Japan with my parents. My big brother is Haru, and Keiko is my little sister.

Once a month we have a sushi evening at our grandparents' home. We all love sushi, and Grandma makes vegetarian ones for Haru, who doesn't eat fish.

Mum always makes my favourite sushi – called maki – to take to Grandma's. Maki is a sushi roll with rice and things like fish, vegetables and egg inside. It's wrapped in dried seaweed, called nori.

While Mum prepares rice, I lay half a sheet of nori on our makisu – that's a mat made of bamboo sticks. I spread warm rice on the nori, leaving a bare strip on the long side. The filling goes down the centre: cucumber or avocado for Haru, and I have salmon. My favourite! Dad likes shrimp with spicy wasabi paste. Too hot for me!

MAKISU

I use the makisu to roll the nori tightly over the filling, then I wet the nori's long edge and keep rolling so it seals the sushi. When the makisu's peeled back, the long roll is firm, ready for slicing.

Sushi has lots of healthy ingredients, and is fresh-tasting and always beautifully presented. This delicious rice dish has become a favourite all over the world.

MAKI SUSHI

Mum wets her knife so rice won't stick to it, and cuts the sushi into little rolls. Then Keiko helps me pack them in a box. We take gari, too – pickled ginger to eat between sushis to freshen our mouths. Gari is sweet and sour and spicy.

GARI

NIGIRI SUSHI

At Grandma's, the table is covered with different types of sushi. They all look wonderful, but I'm glad we brought my favourites!

INDEX

Argentina ... 36–37
bigos ... 40–41
bobotie ... 26–27
bread ... 11, 18, 26–27, 33, 40, 41, 44
breakfast ... 5, 18–19, 30–31
celebrations ... 14–15, 16, 23, 42–43
cheese ... 10–11, 17, 18, 24–25, 29, 39, 44
China ... 34–35
dessert ... 10, 41
dinner ... 16, 21, 23, 24–25, 40–41, 44
dumplings ... 34
eggs ... 9, 15, 24, 26, 27, 36, 46
empanadas ... 36–37
Ethiopia ... 8–9
Fiji ... 42–43
fish ... 20–21, 36, 43, 45, 46–47
France ... 10–11
fruit ... 19, 22, 27, 28–29, 30, 32, 36, 39, 44
garlic ... 9, 10, 11, 13, 22, 23, 27, 34, 36, 39, 43, 44, 45
gelateria ... 28–29
gelato ... 28–29
Germany ... 24–25
Greece ... 18–19
gursha ... 9
Hawaiian pizza ... 17
herbs ... 10, 11, 17, 25, 29, 31, 44, 45
honey ... 19
idli sambar ... 30–31
India ... 30–31
injera ... 8–9
Italy ... 28–29
Jamaica ... 32–33
Japan ... 46–47
jerk chicken ... 32–33
Käsespätzle ... 24–25
kazan ... 22
koulouris ... 18–19
lovo ... 42–43
lunch ... 10–11, 12
Malaysia ... 26
Margherita pizza ... 17
meat ... 9, 11, 17, 22, 23, 26, 27, 32–33, 34, 35, 36, 38, 39, 40, 41, 43, 45
Mexico ... 12–13
Mexico City ... 12–13
meze ... 44–45
mitad ... 8
Netherlands ... 14–15
nuts ... 19, 27, 28, 44, 45
odeng ... 20–21
picnic ... 12–13
pizza ... 16–17
pizzeria ... 16
plov ... 22–23
poffertjes ... 14–15
Poland ... 40–41
ratatouille ... 10–11
rice ... 23, 31, 33, 44, 45, 46, 47
salad ... 10, 11, 23, 39, 45
seafood ... 20–21, 34, 39, 45, 46
snacks ... 5, 12–13, 36–37
South Africa ... 26–27
South Korea ... 20–21
Spain ... 37
spätzles ... 25
spices ... 9, 22, 27, 30, 31, 32–33, 34, 36, 43, 44, 45, 46, 47
sushi ... 46–47
tamalera ... 13
tamales ... 12–13
Turkey ... 44–45
UK ... 32–33
USA ... 16–17
Uzbekistan ... 22–23
vegetables ... 8, 10–11, 22, 25, 29, 30, 31, 32, 33, 34, 35, 36, 39, 40, 41, 45, 46
wonton soup ... 34–35
yogurt ... 19, 44